Turning Pages

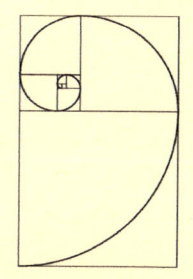

Poems

By: J L Carey Jr.

Agogeebic Press, LLC

Agogeebic Press, LLC, Sunday Lake Street, PO Box 131, Wakefield, MI 49968

http://www.gogebicbooks.com/

A special thanks to Associated Content for previously publishing *Grasping Lineage*, *Flower Picking* and *Easter Morning*.

ISBN-13: **978-0-9822390-5-6** - $12.95

Book design by Broken Cog Media   Cover art: Ink drawing of Japanese Enri Sangaku

Copyright © 2010 by J L Carey Jr

All Rights Reserved. Manufactured in the United States of America. No part of this book may be used or reproduced in any manner whatsoever without written permission except in the case of brief quotations embodied in critical articles and reviews.

Table of Contents

Ichi 3
    Skeleton Mountain 4
    The Vintner 5
    Organizing Parallels 6
    Beautiful Benten 7
    A Wash 8
    Corner Stone 9
    The Ragaraja 10
    Easter Morning 11
    This Time 12
    Eternal Cultivation 13
    August Star 14
    Flower Picking 15
    The Assembly 16
    Vacuum Gliding 17
    Hidden Qualities 18
    Universal Song 19
    Immovable Buddha 20
    13 Ascending 21
    Mystic Downpour 22
    A Principled 23
Ni 24
    The Illusion 25
    Affective Forecast 26
    Brain Signatures 27
    Ecumenical Symbol 28
    Finding Koufuku 29
    Free Will 30
    Genus Volvox 31
    Heaven's Dogs 32
    Earth Tremor 33
    Hinaga Yume 34
    Hydrometer Floating 35
    Koicha Matcha 36
    Morning Fog 37
    Sacramental Crossing 38
    The Restoration 39
    Tsuki Yomi 40
    Vesica Pisces 41

	We Fools	42
	72 %	43
	8 Heads	44
San		45
	Storm Broke	46
	Bed Making	47
	Dividing Rock	48
	Dream Catcher	49
	Eighty Six'd	50
	Equivalence Principle	51
	First Sage	52
	Goose Egg	53
	Kumo Amimono	54
	Land Lord	55
	Natural Light	56
	Single Points	57
	Slate Cleaning	58
	Sousou Noukou	59
	The Exchange	60
	The Tunnel	61
	The Preservation	62
	Xanthous Reflection	63
	Yamabushi's Folly	64
	Bamboo Princes	65
Shi		66
	Initial Derivative	67
	Hebereke Kansou	68
	Butterfly Phenomenon	69
	Chinou Sujichigai	70
	Chuunitsu Sukin	71
	Double Helix	72
	Emergency Scene	73
	Grus Japonensis	74
	Hebi Minshuu	75
	Learning Curve	76
	Once Again	77
	Ripple Effect	78
	Seccond Nature	79
	Grasping Lineage	80
	The Elucidation	81
	The Stick	82
	Untoward Divergence	83
	Varicose Heart	84
	Zero Prefecture	85
	The Encompassment	86

Turning Pages

A world of dew,

And within every dewdrop

A world of struggle

— Kobayashi Issa

For Darlene Chiyomi Carey

Ichi

Skeleton Mountain

High I hear the howl,
Those long gone bones still chanting
In the mountain wind

What appeals whisper?
What fell within that temple
The heart or the soul?

Love can be cruel and timeless.

The faithful abstains,
Though, it's our nature to seek
And to make mistakes

The grave paradox.
A vow to opposition.
Pray, *Ajari - Joan*

The Vintner

Such supple fruit from
Water sweeping eastward winds;
The breath of Bacchus.

Taut vine, its sinews
Stretched, God child, tacked to the tree,
We will drink from you.

Glorious the vintner's task.

Balanced by the oak,
Time beautifies your bouquet;
Sweet slumbering cask.

In metamorphose
There is a longing to breathe;
To intoxicate.

Organizing Parallels

Seed within a seed
These sequences store away
Waiting to spring forth

Infinite in size
Energy, vibrating strings,
Cells, societies

Constant as the Universe

Seeming chaotic
Mysterious, puzzling
This is the design

All things existing
Inside another being
Communal and whole

Beautiful [1]Benten

Amidst the bamboo
At the foot of the mountain
A cherry tree bloomed

Beneath the blossoms
She plucked her [2]*biwa*, luring,
Taming the dragon

Who could resist this Goddess?

A hint of jasmine
Lingered in the bed of white;
Simple petals fall.

Poor wandering priest,
Your serpent loosed then handled,
Never stood a chance.

---

[1] Benten – Japanese Goddess of love, music and poetry who is often depicted riding the dragon she tamed.
[2] Biwa - Japanese short-necked fretted lute often played by Benten.

A Wash

Small and simple shell
Beached for albatross to mock
Vacant and bleaching

Perhaps sojourners
In kinder more polished days
Will retrieve this conch

Marveling in its spiral

A lover's treasure
Regarded, ornamental,
Worn for all to see,

To touch, feel, listen
The whisper, oceans wisdom
Ancient and distilled

Corner Stone

One is the basis
Perspectives vanishing point
The eyes illusion

One and One begins
Moves. A visible unit
Progressing forward

This embryonic [3]*Uchuu*

Tandem travelers
Pioneers on the set course
To complexity

Tender and rhythmic
They breed multitudinous
Towards perfection

---

[3] Uchuu – Japanese for Universe or cosmos.

The [4]Ragaraja

Sweet [5]*Aizen Myoo*
With grossly good intention
Sewed those timeworn seeds

His lion then tore
The virgin from his virtues
While the third eye wept

Enlightening them alike

Love, as a mountain,
Will withstand the elements
Seemingly secure.

Sudden eruption
Though, claims the bones of many
A passionate soul.

---

[4] Ragaraja - Buddist King of passion, also know as Aizen Myoo.
[5] Aizen Myoo – Japanese God of love, depicted with a lion's head and a third eye.

Easter Morning

Life springs from past life.
The fresh green blades of grass blaze
With sunlit dewdrops

A dove selects sticks,
Her belly laden with eggs
As she basket weaves;

Every molecule on cue.

Earth's clockwork code,
Like a time release capsule;
Patient and precise.

Inhale, know, exhale.
Something died so we could live,
A most precious trade.

This Time

It comes and leaves us
Like oxygen from our lungs,
Sure, yet unnoticed.

Inexplicable
Such infinite existence
And whence was the start?

This time, our strange privilege

Locked somewhere between
The ever unfolding now
And dissolving past

We alone use its
Archival ability
To map history.

Eternal Cultivation

Love will alter life;
Transfiguring those who taste
Like [6]*Seiobo's* peach.

Her gorgeous orchard,
Ripe with the sweet flesh of fruit,
Titillating buds,

Penetrating the spirit,

Holding, suspending
That fresh flavor on the tongue.
Immortalizing,

Ingraining passion
As the body absorbs it
So instinctively.

---

[6]   Seiobo – An immortal Sennin or mountain spirit of Japan known as the Queen Mother of the West who has a garden of peaches, which, only blossoms once every 1000 years. Those that eat a peach become immortal.

August Star

Ominous black hole
Lurking like a midnight thief
Bent on stealing souls

Beware this machine
Dark industrious nightmare
Lures then devours

Its grim eyes piercing the heart

Devil of the void
[7]Amatsu – Mikaboshi
Cloaked shade of shadows

Extinguishing light
The ruined twisting in his mouth
Slaves to the abyss

---

[7] Amatsu – Mikaboshi – Japanese god of evil.

Flower Picking

Fanciful organ
Always a source of pleasure
And trouble as well.

Wisteria blooms
Stripping away all senses.
Passion is mindless

Stay men. Stay your wants and needs.

There is more to life
Than aimless florid conquest,
And ill-fated risk.

A moment for what?
This field is full of pitfalls,
Leave it for the fools.

The Assembly

Within the stone walls
Those capricious Gods gathered
Devising beneath

Canopies of trees
The fate of a mortal's heart,
That fragile tissue

Mettle gone *twitterpated*

Joyfully they mused
To bring *Ajari - Joan* down
From his moss green crags

Laughing as he strayed
[8]Izumo's gullet shaking
One's pain their pleasure.

---

[8] Izumo – An old providence of Japan named for the Goddess Izanami, Mother of Japan.

Vacuum Gliding

What wind blows this mill?
Propelling old, synergic
Antiquarians

Celestial gust
Orbs, worlds, sails on the rotor
Ethereal pinions

This engine ever cranking

The wise draw from it
Harnessing that energy
In its raw essence

Nude, [9]*Chokaro* smiles
Conscious he's grit in the swirl
Of inanity

---

[9] Chokaro – A Japanese Sennin or spirit known for traveling. He carried a magic pumpkin and if he blew into it out came a horse.

Hidden Qualities

We are lacklusters
Spinning in the tumbler
Aching for polish

Seeking through the rough
Combing on the coarse beach
Traversing mountains

Or the dark womb of heaven

New and old alike
Recycle through the ages
Dateless collectors

Archeologists
Unearthing *Ajari - Joan*
By digging inwards

Universal Song

What melodies this?
These strange notes play within us
Beneath everything

Subatomic keys
Harmonize through the cosmos
And the Maestro God

Sweet the orchestral rhythm

Pure, vast, unending
This music, this arrangement
Materialized

We experience
In living composition
You and I a chord

Immovable Buddha

Primordial fount
Rich [10]*Ashuku - Nyorai*
Precious and giving

We arise from you
As the land does from the sea
Beautiful and proud

Majestic elemental

Ever revolving
Ever evolving, churning
On the fixed axis

Making manifest
That mysterious design
Of our fathers hand

---

[10] Ashuku – Nyorai – The element of Earth in Japanese cosmology.

13 Ascending

Under the timber
At thirteen hundred meters
The creature collapsed

His feet, chewed and raw,
Had come upon the coarse teeth
Of an old pinecone

Crushing the curious pod

A moments distract
But the end in tact caught both
The sole and wonder

This golden sequence
That unfolds counter clockwise
And clockwise as well

Mystic Downpour

The wind rushed cool rain
Venting the scent of earthworm,
That crawling death fume

A distinct ground must
Corrupting the atmosphere
And yet you inhaled

Savored it like cellared wine

Smelling, tasting it,
The senses saturating
With the green gray clouds

A strange communion
Pooling in shallow puddles,
Soaking the marrow

A Principled

So, *Ajari – Joan*
Returned to that primal state
In absent reason

Wandering wildly
As any rogue creature might
Less a priori

This rudimentary man

Pacing his mountain
Of vacant thought and dismal
Leeching woebegones

Malady ridden
As syphilis rode Nietzsche
To a God like death

Ni

The Illusion

On the spiral stair
You stand at the half way point
Looking down the coil

It appears smaller
At the base of the first flight
And just above you

The well seems even larger

Yet, beyond this floor
Each grows tinier until
Equally tapered.

Both ends trick the eye.
The mind understands the ruse
But, wants to believe.

Affective Forecast

When he took his vows
His mind filled with glorious
Anticipations

A future wrought with
Spiritual happiness
And enlightenment

But expectations deceive

And [11]*yosou* failed him
For who could ever really know
What life has in store?

This *impact bias*
Setting our emotions up
To be deflated

---

[11] Yosou – Japanese for expectation or forecast.

Brain Signatures

In the astral plain
His memories nestled in
To that black velvet

As though heaven were
But a dreamy down blanket
For their recounting

That brush of the kettles steam

Her beautiful words
And the soft touch of her smooth skin
So lightly perfumed

From this other side,
Of a darkness he perceived,
All things were alight

Ecumenical Symbol

Follow the [12]*enri*
To understand unity
In the unending

Mark the [13]*sangaku*
To evidence the journey
And instruct the page

Knowledge circles back around

Finding new spirits
In the vast mothering sphere
Of blues and sages

This event cradle
From which all things originate
And return again

---

[12] Enri – The circle principle of Japanese Mathematics or Wasan.
[13] Sangaku – A custom in Japan of presenting mathematical problems on wooden tablets, primarily found hanging outside if Shinto shrines.

Finding [14]Koufuku

In the firmament
The waning priests prayer drifted
To a gentle ear

The well-rounded God
Reclined against his rice bag
In full reverence

While the playful cherubs laughed

Smiling, [15]*Hotei* said:
Be content with a full plate
For excess is waste

There is happiness
In that which is before you
Desire nothing more

---

[14] Koufuku – Japanese for happiness or blessedness.
[15] Hotei – Japanese God of laughter, happiness and contentment. Usually depicted as a laughing fat man carrying a bag of rice and children.

Free Will

There are natural
Causal effects and factors
That we try to rule

Holding in our mind
The desire to be more
Than archaic *wight*

This exercising of choice

To elevate us
Towards that divinity
We hold as sacred

But, the law is firm
And ours is not above cause
We belong to it

[16]*Genus Volvox*

What is the body
But nothing more than clusters
Of *simbiose* cells

In this coupling
There is a [17]*mokuteki*
That is realized

The numerous forming one

Purpose built beings,
Vehicles for the spirit
To experience

Strange mechanisms
Or matter of no matter
For our disposal

---

[16] Genus Volvox - Minute pale green flagellates occurring in tiny spherical colonies; minute flagella rotate the colony about an axis.
[17] Mokuteki – Japanese for purpose, goal or objective.

Heaven's Dogs

Each sotted morning
On the path to the summit
The [18]*tangu* emerged

Their long beaks taunting,
Chiding him, as demons do,
While his wits wandered

Strangely keeping him on course

Those ebony crows
With wings spread like scarab guides
To the afterworld

Guarding that worn trail
Of winding smoke and madness
Till his way was clear

---

[18] Tangu – Mountain spirits of Japan usually carved out of wood and depicted as birds or priest-like creatures. Initially they came from heaven, became demons and then evolved to mischievous but helpful spirits.

Earth Tremor

As he left her home
She took the cherry blossom
From her long black hair

Whirling the flower
With those delicate fingers
While her soft cheeks blushed

Then rested it in his hand

The virile lifelines
Trembling and then folding
As if the weight were

Unendurable
Fracturing his world along
The new faults that formed

[19]Hinaga [20]Yume

The meat plow threw her
Into that disheveled state
Along the wayside

The deer lay solid,
It seemed, for several days
But at last passing

All save the face picked bone clean

Left in that long dream
Aspirations reflecting
In her souls mirrors

Life plans persisting
Until the darling maggots
Lovingly ate them

---

[19] Hinaga – Japanese for longday.
[20] Yume – Japanese for dream.

Hydrometer Floating
For Chiyoko Bruce

Her memory was
Sweet and inebriating
Like fresh Lambrusco

Deep mauve and warming
To those debilitated
Motoring senses

A timeless thought fermented

As though the brain were
Comprised of luscious sugars
In constant exchange

And as it savored
He drifted in the dreamy
Must of nostalgia

[21]Koicha Matcha

She poured the sweet tea
Jasmine steaming from the bowl
Of hot green tonic

The unlikely mix
Blending quite naturally
As the kettle boiled

Subtle gestures move mountains

Charcoal glowing red
The bamboo ladle resting
While their eyes engaged

And when he left her
His heart remained there marking
The ends beginning

---

[21] Koitcha Matcha – A thick sweet tea from Japan often used in tea ceremonies.

Morning Fog

Through thinning [22]*kiri*
The dank smell of pine needles
Climbed in the air

Blending with the song
Of robins and warblers
Hidden in the bush

Ants caravanned unmindful

As did the coy that
Traveled with grace and silence
Below the water

Whose surface mirrored
The shimmering Ivory
Of love and ruin

---

[22] Kiri – Japanese for fog or mist.

Sacramental Crossing

Petals and microbes
Whirled in the cleansing current
Of the mountain stream

On the bank crosswise
[23]*Sojobo* waited calmly
As the willows swayed

Reflecting in the water

While the wading priest
Stirred up soot and slimy stones
With each pressing step

Reaching the king who
Warmly held that atavist
Soul to his bosom

---

[23] Sojobo – The elderly King of the Yamabushi Tengu, depicted with white hair.

The Restoration

The old man sat down
His weary marrow resting
On [24]*Hakkotsu – San*

Calming the turmoil
That had twisted in his mind
For unnumbered years

Scattered wits crystallizing

Forming coherence
Under the tall swaying pines
That combed the blue sky

Pleasant tears dropping
While the echoing breath left
In supplication

---

[24] Hakkotsu – San – Japanese for Skeleton Mountain.

[25]Tsuki Yomi

Wax Midnight drifter -
Tethered orb in the darkness
Pallid and mournful

One ever questions
How this sibling rivalry
Hangs so in the air?

God's and men both suffer sins

Tired you wane again
Falling with the bruised heaven
Never to face her

Night and day at odds
No olive branch could extend
So far a chasm

---

[25] Tsuki Yomi – The God of the Moon, born out of the right eye of Izanaki, who, after insulting his sister Amaterasu, was banished to the other side of the world so that she would never have to see him again.

Vesica Pisces

The smell of almond
Swam in the mothering breeze,
Like playful dolphins.

Ajari - Joan reeled,
Lost in heaven's [26]*mandorla*,
As did [27]Osiris

When [28]Isis devoured him.

Drawing from that well,
Her divine words whispering
Hot on his right ear,

Islands erupting,
Swelling from this Marina
Of vestal glory.

---

[26] Mandorla – Italian for almond, it is an ancient symbol of two circles overlapping one another to form an almond shape or Vesica Pisces in the center. It is representative of the three phases of the moon or Goddesses of the moon, the sacred feminine and is widely known as the Jesus Fish.
[27] Osiris – Egyptian God of life, death and fertility.
[28] Isis - Egyptian Goddess and wife of Osiris.

We Fools

As his energy
Lifted up above the globe
All truths were revealed

The warn vehicle
Disintegrated in prayer
As pine seeds flourished

Drawing that which he released

The saplings springing
While birds, insects and microbes
Gained his sustenance

A fool no longer
Ajari - Joan realized
He was home again

72 %

The human body
Is composed primarily
Of liquid water

Every droplet
Has passed through an animal
At various times

Just as it has rained to earth

Recycling on,
Filtering through sand and soil,
Evaporating

Reconstituting,
Taking on some living form
As it has before

8 Heads

When *Ajari - Joan*
Was baited by that [29]*hana*
In boggling bloom

All of life's forces,
Both natural and divine,
Acted in concert

A trap timed to perfection

And so he fell prey
Just as Izumo's serpent
Did to [30]*Susanoh*

Its several heads
All taken in as easily
By like enticements

---

[29] Hana – Japanese for flower.
[30] Susanoh – Wild Japanese Shinto god of the winds, storms, oceans, and snakes who was exiled from heaven. Later he would redeem himself by killing the eight-headed serpent or Hydra, which allowed him to marry the princess Kusinada. He is also attributed with building the Izumo shrine.

San

Storm Broke

The typhoon spiraled
As the two strong systems clashed
In blind violence

Those ancient forces
Vague as the essence of time
Gripped in twisting rage

Love caught in their tempests eye

As the waves destroyed
And the wild winds tore away
What had stood so proud

Leaving that temple
But a grisly skeleton
Of its former self

Bed Making

In the crystal stream,
Enraptured with thoughts of him,
The coy goddess bathed

Cleansing her body
As her current thoughts drifted
To that carnal place

Within the cherry blossoms

But the weather fowled
And the wind swept all away
So upon return

Found her bed empty
Save a broken black flower
On that hallowed ground

Dividing Rock

When love's forbidden
Insanity takes the mind
And all matter's lost

Like [31] *Izanaki*
When in that terrible state
Sought [32] *Izanami*

Disregarding her warning

Her dreadful body
Deep within the underworld
Riddled with decay

And so the priest went
Headlong to his dear's embrace
Arms espousing fate

---

[31] Izanaki – Primordial God of the world and co-creator of the Japanese Islands who, after losing his wife Izanami, went to the underworld to retrieve her, despite her telling him not to. After seeing his wife's terrible condition he blocked the entrance to the underworld with a giant rock.

[32] Izanami – Primordial Goddess of the world and co-creator of the Japanese Islands who died after baring her son, the God of Fire.

Dream Catcher
For Vanna Lyons

The curved red willow
Held seven webbed sinews tight
Across its wicket

Waiting to ensnare
Those insignificant dreams
Or ill willed nightmares

Guarding the darks unconscious

Strung in the window
Like a gate at the portal
Of reality

This [33]*yume ami*
Weeding out malevolence
With the morning light

---

[33] Yume ami – Japanese for dream net.

Eighty Six'd

For the desperate
Living with tremendous loss
Can feel like drowning

As though their footings
Been engulfed by a dark sea
Of fear and anguish

Flooding the powerless soul

Suffocating them
As they slip further below
The murky deluge

An Ark-less hatful –
And so *Ajari - Joan* flailed
While the tide deepened

Equivalence Principle

What the eye perceives
Is not necessarily
A reality

A line that seems straight
May truly be skewed or curved
As light through space-time

A disorienting path

Though, careful plotting
May bring a desired result,
In many cases

One can never know,
With unbending certainty,
Where their path will lead

First Sage

With the intellect
Knowledge permeates the mind
As water does sand

Filtering through it,
Purifying as it goes
To the aquifer

Volumes of information

Stored for our employ
Just as great [34]*Thales* so divined
His solar eclipse

By tapping into
The reservoir he'd absorbed
So efficiently

---

[34] Thales - A pre-Socratic Greek philosopher and one of the Seven Sages. Regarded by many as the first philosopher in the Greek tradition as well as the "father of science".

Goose Egg
For Grace Anne Carey

Now – does not exist
It is but a symbolic
Representation

Just as zero is
On the numerical line
Of mathematics

Something depicting nothing

For everything
That beings experience
Takes place in the past

As though time unfolds
In strangely cyphered
Delayed reactions

[35]*Kumo Amimono*

Morning dew shimmers
On the complex spider web
Woven in the grass

The intricate trap
Entangling sunlight, eyes
And a world of thoughts

A miniature vortex

Spun instinctively
According to the blueprints
Threaded in and out

Moored, framed and spiraled
To catch these souls in the wind
Of life's happenstance

---

[35] Kumo Amimono – Japanese for spider web.

Land Lord

There, in the priest's path,
Stood that infamous red boar
Its sharp tusks gleaming

Eyes blazing wildly
With the blood of [36]*Adonis*
Searing in the flames

Insane with its killing lust

And so it advanced
As [37]*Ohkuni - nushi*'s tree
Opened and took him

Into its hollow
Where he was hid safe until
The devil had gone

---

[36] Adonis – A Greek mythological figure born out of tree when a bore struck it with its tusks. This was considered a foreshadowing of his death. Later, a wild boar killed Adonis while he was hunting it. He is also an annually-renewed, ever-youthful vegetation god, a life-death-rebirth deity whose nature is tied to the calendar.

[37] Ohkuni – Nushi – Japanese God of the Earth, also known as the Lord of the Land, who was re-born out of a tree after his brothers tricked him into a boar hunt.

Natural Light

The sky was soft blue
Like some angelic ocean
Warmed with summer rays

Suspended mid air
White clouds huddled in layers
Of still cumulous

Plush pillows for day drifting

While low in the shade
A black dog relieved itself
As the page observed

And the multitudes
Rushed without understanding
Or concern for not

Single Points

The consequences
Of particular actions
Can always be linked

Like *Ajari - Joan*
We proceed from one outcome
To yet another

All of them interwoven

Entwining us all
In this defining meshwork
Of conjoined events

Legacy morsels
Wrapped up and tucked away for
Later digestion

Slate Cleaning
For William Bruce

It's speculated
That all the cosmic knowledge
Is retained at birth

Some also assume
This wisdom is forgotten
As we are informed

So called facts replacing truths

A sad perversion
This ease in which they escape
Our flatulent minds

Erased forever
Like countless chalked equations
Wiped from the blackboard

[38]*Sousou Noukou*

The fog hugged the earth
With a low silent blanket
Of precipitant

Until the sun rose
Gently evaporating
The mourning moisture

Exposing what was unseen

Those tall wild flowers
And a cautious doe grazing
In the lush meadow

Birds uprooting worms
Beneath rows of lawn clippings
And a day sky moon

---

[38] Sousou Noukou – Japanese for early density.

The Exchange

And so [39]*Ho-ori*
Harkened back to the mountain
He had left before

His mind beclouded
With [40]*Hoderi's* sunken hook
And unforgivings

Pettiness takes precedence

But near the clear stream
The old man rose and bid him
Return to that sea

Where he fell in love
With [41]*Toyotama-hime*
Just as fate divined

---

[39] Ho-ori – Mythological Japanese figure and ancestor to the emperors of Japan. Legend states that Ho-ori lost his brother Hoderi's fishing hook after borrowing it. His brother would not forgive him for it so Ho-ori went to the bottom of the sea to try and find it. There he met the Sea Gods daughter Toyotama-hime and they fell in love.
[40] Hoderi – Brother of Ho-ori.
[41] Toyotama-hime – Princess daughter of the sea god, Ryūjin.

The Tunnel

A light penetrates
The solitude and darkness
Of your fetal state

And though unaware
Of where this beacon ushers
You know to follow

Exiting to existence

Taking your due place
Among the countless others
Who've marked the time-line

Until, exhausted,
You close your eyes to find
A light there once more

The Preservation

Five Millennia
Covered and enshrouded those
Valdaron Lovers

Still locked in embrace
As though time had petrified
The tragic union

Shakespearean archetypes

Their arms espousing,
An arrow lodged in his spine
And one in her side

Cupid's handy work
Immortalized and unearthed
For all to esteem

Xanthous Reflection

The yellowish orb
Surfaced at the ocean's edge
Burning her image

Onto the blue skin
Of that pulsating body
Like an aerie brand

Beautifully didactic

And on the cool beach
Faint morning swells rushed ashore
In rolling cadence

While a young priest sat,
His white new robe emblazoned
With what lay ahead

[42]Yamabushi's Folly

Opening his eyes
Ajari - Joan found the tree
Stripped of its flowers

And as the petals
Scattered in the naked wind
A chill cut his skin

For it seemed his love had left

Thus filling his mind
With grief and disillusion
For this misleading

And so he drifted
Leaving the token he'd worn
Strewn upon the soil

---

[42] Yanmabushi - Japanese mountain priests and ascetics.

Bamboo Princess
For Tabbitha Hisayo Carey

All things are like rain –
Droplets brought forth and released
To the atmosphere

Invariably
Retroverting to the well
Of their origin

As [43]*Kaguya – Hime* did

Escaping as light
From the surface of Luna
To the bamboo fields

Until angelic
Soldiers sadly took her home
To that orb again

---

[43] Kaguya – Hime – Japanese mythological figure and and oldest narrative of Japan about a Bamboo princess from the moon. She is found as an infant in a stalk of bamboo and is raised by the childless bamboo cutter and his wife. The princess is loved dearly, but after she is grown, upon a full moon, soldiers take her back to the moon against her will.

Shi

Initial Derivative

When time first inhaled
Particles coaxed and courted
As all lover's will

Until they united
Clinging in that strange embrace
Of procreation

Natural as the breath was

Joining and parting
While the new cloud expanded
Multiplicative

In his wondrous eyes
A phantasmagoric glint
Then the priest exhaled

[44]*Hebereke* [45]*Kansou*

In the drunken stars
Bending quantum thoughts raced out
At the speed of light

Belligerently
Provoking like particles
In the dark matter

Shooting the rotation curve

Like splayed champagne corks
Fired Apollo rocket style
To where but God knows

Until they came home
Splashing in the deep comfort
Of yesterday dreams

---

[44] Hebereke – Japanese for drunk.
[45] Kansou - Japanese for thoughts.

Butterfly Phenomenon

The two lovers kissed
As blossoms fell around them
In the stirring wind

A causal outcome
That riffled from the root source
Like an a-bomb wave

Altering all in its path

Moving and changing
The position of the earth
And solar system

While the sun's polls flipped
Then settled in again for
The next eleven

[46]*Chinou Sujichigai*

*[47]Dogs will returneth
To the pools of their vomit
As fools to folly*

And so the priest went
Discarding his vows again
For the heart is head

Muscle subject to reflex

An unconscious act
Stimulated by her tea
Like some strange potion

A tonic devised
To grip the young mans logic
And prompt his yielding

---

[46] Chinou Sujichigai – Japanese for brain cramp.
[47] Proverb 26:11 from the Bible.

[48]Chuunitsu Sukin

Through the blue heaven
Under wind and wing of crane
His prayers flew further

Until they nested
In [49]Jurojin's ancient ear
Like migrant warblers

Screeching with insanity

And so the god spoke
With happiness in his heart -
Be not bewildered

[50]Life deals many blows
This is why an old tortoise
Carries a thick shell

---

[48] Chuunitsu Sukin – Japanese for thick skinned.
[49] Jurojin - Japanese God of longevity and happiness in old age. His attributes are a tortoise and a crane.
[50] Chinese proverb.

Double Helix

*[51] Wisdom and virtue,
Like the two wheels of a cart,
Work in unison*

Each complimenting
The other by carrying
An equal burden

Virtue in turn with wisdom

Twining together
As a pair of strands will form
A durable rope

That holds and dispels
All that's good and right between
Wisdom and virtue

---

[51] Japanese proverb.

Emergency Scene

In the lane ahead
Lights swirled as paramedics
Marked the time of death

Those rigorous hands
Still clutching the steering wheel
As the car idled

The new road fixed in his eyes

Describing something
Holy different than that
Facial expression

The agape jaw locked
And cheek muscles spasming
While the heart rested

[52]*Grus Japonensis*

A subtle snow fell
Blanketing *Ajari – Joan*
As his bones shivered

And through the vapor
Of his warm breath he spied
Two courting Red-Crowns

Their long black necks intertwined

A ritual dance
That endured the grind of time
And encroaching man

Enkindling thoughts
Of past ephemeral joys
So long forsaken

---

[52] Grus Japonensis - The Japanese crane, also known as the red-crowned crane is sacred and seen as a symbol of fidelity, good luck, love and long life. It is also an endangered species and the second rarest crane species in the world.

[53]Hebi Minshuu

In the agape door
Of that dark dismal temple
The cold wind whipped

Loves lifeless body
Her hand still clenching the priests
Broken black flower

Unwinding his sanity

As the callous snake
[54]*Yaichiro* slithered out from
That vacant socket

Hissing - there's always
A serpent in the shadows
Poised to strike… my friend

---

[53] Hebi Minshuu – Japanese for snake people.
[54] Yaicharo – Japanese Mythology about a man scorned by his lover. He then died from a broken heart and became a snake. Later he killed the woman and was seen slithering out of her eye socket.

Learning Curve

Producing more yield
While expending less time seems
The [55]*Wright* thing to do

For basic creatures
Will become more efficient
Through repetition

Experience thus makes us

So the wise will find
[56]*To teach is also to learn*
A two-fold practice

Perpetuating
Quantity and quality
With maturation

---

[55] T.P. Wright – Deisigned a model known as the learning curve or experience curve and is based on the simple idea that the time required to perform a task decreases as a worker gains experience.
[56] German Proverb.

Once Again

Key vibrato strings
Hydrogen and oxygen
Blending and parting

Amino acids
Structuring then dividing
Colonies of cells

Making us and shaping us

Animal machines
Living and undergoing
Final exhaustion

Decomposition
Preparing our reunion
With *Ajari – Joan*

Ripple Effect

Her love was a stone
Cast into the reservoir
Of the young mans life

Disturbing the still
Serenity of his heart,
Body and psyche

His faculties disrupted

As the ripples rolled
Deforming the idea
He held of himself

[57]*For one cannot see*
The mirror of their image
In running water

---

[57] Japanese proverb.

Second Nature

Time will rightly show
[58]*The rule of virtue is not*
Knowing but doing

Thus the river goes
And wisely follows the path
Of least resistance

So the page must take action

Putting into use
The wisdom that has been endowed
To their able hands

Until it becomes
Instinctively effortless
Reflexive motion

---

[58] Socratic Philosophy.

Grasping Lineage
For my Dad and Lucas

There's something greater
Than the hearts pleasure passing
Through their holding hands

The simple gesture
Unfolding like a silent
Changing of the guards

Their like particles bonding

Michael Angelo
Couldn't have created a
Painting more touching

This time old exchange
Of loves replenishment, of
Immortality

The Elucidation

The graven embraced
As his humble words spiraled
From the mountains horn

Beholding below
The worn and withering shell
That housed and drove him

As any good machine would

And all around him
A vaporous light billowed
In ethereal birth

Juxtaposing paths
Ajari - Joan transcended
Beginning and end

The Stick

The fly lay frozen;
Trapped in that struggling pose
Atop the butter

Its delicate wings
Glued against the salt and lard
Of its enticer

As though spread out for display

Warning the others
Of the delicious folly
It had indulged in

Grimly reminding
That we all will make mistakes
But can choose not to

Untoward Divergence

Ajari –Joan wept
While her crying went muted
By the mountain wind

Only yards between
Separated the two souls
Lost within the pines

The trees groaning as they swayed

[59]*For adversity*
Is the heartless foundation
Of life and virtue

And so they drifted
Farther from one another
As their minds despaired

---

[59] Japanese Proverb.

Varicose Heart

[60]*Love was a thorn*
Festering in the old priests
Tainted emotions

Debilitating
As memories of her churned
In his aging mind

A sea roiling in a storm

Of could have should have
And arduous repentance
Over a choice made

And indecisions
Languishing on Limbo's edge
Ready to be reached

---

[60] Irish Proverb – "Even a small thorn causes festering".

Zero Prefecture

All is connected
And nothing is important
In the grand design

Worries are worthless,
Opportunities endless
And needless as well

Fate is love and hate its poise

Religions, morals,
Philosophies and science
Are but opinions

And if all ended,
What would be left to miss this
Grand conjuration?

The Encompassment

Look. There. Just ahead,
Ajari – Joan waits for us,
Longing for embrace.

In this comforting
Full revolution is seen;
The turn's conclusion;

God at the pivotal point.

All we've ever sought
Has been centripetally
Leading us around,

Towards discernment;
The shell removed exposing,
Finally, our tale.

J L Carey Jr. is a writer and an artist living in Michigan with his wife and three children. He holds an MFA in Creative Writing from National University and a BA in English from the University of Michigan with a concentration in writing. He has had various stories and poems published in both print and online journals.